Images of War

Hitler's Tank Killer

The Sturmgeschütz at War 1940-1945

Hans Seidler

Pen & Sword
MILITARY

First published in Great Britain in 2010 by
PEN & SWORD MILITARY
an imprint of
Pen & Sword Books Ltd,
47 Church Street,
Barnsley,
South Yorkshire.
S70 2AS

A CIP record for this book is available from the British Library.

ISBN 978 1 84884 174 4

Printed and bound by CPI UK

Pen & Sword Books Ltd incorporates the imprints of
Pen & Sword Aviation, Pen & Sword Maritime, Pen & Sword Military,
Wharncliffe Local History, Pen & Sword Select, Pen & Sword Military Classics,
Leo Cooper, Remember When, Seaforth Publishing and Frontline Publishing

For a complete list of Pen & Sword titles please contact
Pen & Sword Books Limited
47 Church Street, Barnsley, South Yorkshire, S70 2AS, England
E-mail: enquiries@pen-and-sword.co.uk
Website: www.pen-and-sword.co.uk

Contents

Introduction 5

Chapter One
From France to Russia 1940-1942 7

Chapter Two
***Ost* Front 1942-1943** 57

Chapter Three
On the Defensive 1943-1944 87

Chapter Four
The Demise of the *Sturmgeschütz* 1944-1945 118

Camouflage and Zimme 147

Typical Assault Gun Unit November 1942 151

Standard StuG.III Varients 152

Sturmgeschütz Units in the Waffen-SS 157

Divisions 157

Introduction

Drawing on a rare collection of German photographs with in depth captions and text, the book tells the story of the *Sturmgeschütz* at war. It provides an absorbing insight into the development, success and demise of the assault gun on the battlefield. Used primarily at first to support infantry as they advanced through France, the Balkans and then Russia, the book shows how these potent weapons of World War Two evolved into tank killers, scoring sizable successes against the growing might of the Red Army. However, as the war turned against the Germans in 1942 designers began producing and fielding new types of *Sturmgeschütz* which were up-gunned and heavily armoured to meet the developing threat.

Eventually some fifty-five percent of the Panzerwaffe comprised of assault guns in order to compensate for the lack of tanks and many of the Panzer and Panzergrenadier divisions. They were now found in numerous units including the divisions and brigades of the *Waffen-SS*, *Wehrmacht* and *Luftwaffe* divisions which had their own assault gun units like the famous Herman Goring Panzer-Korps. *Panzerjäger* units of the various divisions also received their own assault gun units. Yet in spite drastic attempts to alleviate of the overall problems in the Panzerwaffe, there were too few assault guns to prevent the overwhelming might of the Red Army, and as a consequence incurred high losses.

An early photograph of a StuG.III accompanied by its crew during a training operation in the early spring of 1940. The origins of the assault guns, or *Sturmgeschütz*, initially lay in German artillery demands for an armoured vehicle that had armour piercing and high explosive capabilities and could provide instant attacking infantry fire support.

Chapter One

From France to Russia
1940-1942

The first time the *Sturmgeschütz* assault gun or StuG made its operational debut was during the French campaign in the summer of 1940. For the concept of *Blitzkrieg* to work effectively tacticians knew that the shock of the advance and a high level of artillery support were vital in any rapid ground operation. During the 1930's the bulk of Germany's heavy artillery were still pulled by animal draught, and it was realized that if *Blitzkrieg* was ever to work effectively without advancing tanks and motorized infantry outstripping artillery support, they required an artillery gun that could be deployed quickly so that vital time was not lost.

Tacticians decided that in order for the artillery to play a prominent part in the new mobile warfare and remain operating in close contact to the battle zone, they needed a highly mobile artillery piece. The new assault gun would be able to keep pace with the mechanized infantry, afford the gunners a degree of armoured protection, and provide support on the battlefield at short notice. An armoured tracked mobile gun was thought to be the best resolution to the problem that could provide close artillery support to the advancing infantry.

In 1936 the first prototype was produced by the Alkett Company. However, the final vehicle was constructed on the chassis of a Pz.Kpfw.III with a 7.5cm short barreled gun. Additional space was achieved by not having a turret and attaching the gun on a fixed mount with a limited traverse.

The StuG had a crew of four: the commander, driver, loader and gunner. Although the vehicle was cramped the assault gun had enough room to officially house 44 rounds. However, the crew found by stacking the ammunition they could carry 90 rounds. This meant they could stay in action longer and able to give the advancing infantry vital support for longer periods.

In June 1940 some 30 StuG's were made readily available for the French campaign. The first *Sturmgeschütz* acquitted themselves well and were organized into independent battalions. Each battalion was composed of three troops, which had six guns each.

At a training ground an early StuG.III can be seen. In 1939 this vehicle rolled off the production line. It was armed with a 7.5cm KwK L/24 gun and was installed in a fixed superstructure on the chassis of a Pz.Kpfw.III tank.

Official regulations stipulated the assault gun was to be employed on the battlefield en masse, and during the French and later the Balkan campaign this was able to be achieved with maximum efficiency. However, one of the shortcomings of the early StuG's was the fact they did not have any machine gun for local defence, and it would not be until late 1941 during the grueling months in Russia that this was finally rectified.

It was in the Soviet Union that the assault guns saw significant development in combating the ever growing might of the Red Army. In Russia, as it had done previously in the Balkans and France, the assault artillery's main objective was to support the infantry in their attacks.

During the first weeks of the invasion of the Soviet Union the StuG.III once again performed extremely well, and after a month of victorious progress, its units found itself fighting on a front 1,000 miles wide. German armour had exploited the terrain and concerted such a series of hammer blows to the Red Army that German tacticians thought it was only a matter of time before the campaign would be over. Yet in spite these successes both *Wehrmacht* and *Waffen-SS* formations were only thinly spread out. Although the armoured spearheads were still achieving rapid victories on all fronts, supporting units were often not keeping pace with them. Consequently, it became increasingly difficult to keep the Panzers supplied with fuel. And without fuel the drive would ground to a halt. Whilst the assault guns remained in close contact with the infantry and were unhindered by the rapid drive, they were slowly deprived of local fire support from the Panzers. As a direct result the StuG became increasingly embroiled in heavy

Another early production StuG.III parked at a training ground in early 1940. The Ausf.A was the first variant of StuG.III to enter service and this was powered by a 300bhp Maybach HL120 TRM V12-cylinder petrol engine, which had a maximum speed of 28mph, and a maximum cross-country speed of 12mph. Since the StuG was primarily designed as a close support weapon for infantry, this speed, especially across country, was deemed more than fast enough.

Two officers with a StuG crew member can be seen with their early production StuG.III variant. It would not be until the spring of 1940 that a series of production models underwent a number of extensive trials with five army batteries, one of which was to participate in the battle of France that year.

fighting and were continually called upon for offensive and defensive fire support which consequently caused a series of high losses in a number of units. Gradually, units were compelled to operate increasingly in an anti-tank role, which were depriving infantry of local fire support.

Problems were made worse when on 6 October the first snowfall of the approaching winter was reported. It melted quickly, but turned the dirt roads into quagmires and rivers into raging torrents. The Russian Autumn with its heavy rain, sleet and snow had arrived, and the armoured drive east began to slow. Wheeled vehicles soon became stuck in a sea of mud and could only advance with the aid of tracked vehicles towing them. No preparations had been made for the winter and Panzer and assault gun units lacked the most basic supplies for cold weather. There were no chains available for towing vehicles, and no anti-freeze for the engines coolant systems. Armoured crewmen and infantrymen alike had no winter clothing either.

At a training camp in 1940 and the crew of a StuG.III can be seen sitting on the engine deck of the vehicle. Parked near to the StuG is a Pz.Kpfw.II. The StuG would soon see its debut on the Western Front and prove a versatile weapon for providing attacking infantry fire support.

In blizzards and temperatures, which fell to 30 degrees below zero, the exhausted Panzer and assault gun units soon run out of fuel and ammunition, and were compelled to break off their attack within sight of Moscow. On 6 December all plans to capture the Russian capital in 1941 had to be abandoned.

To make matters worse assault gun crews soon realized how limited their weapons were against the Russian T-34 and KW tanks that were beginning to be seen in ever greater numbers. By late 1941 assault guns had taken on a vital anti-tank role but crews soon found-out to their surprise that the armour piercing ammunition they were using was useless in long distance firing. Instead crew had to fight Soviet tanks at suicidal close combat distances, and still found it necessary to fire four or even five shots to score one successful hit.

This technical inferiority coupled with the fact that the first winter on the Eastern Front had hindered any large-scale operations ensured that the assault gun was severely limited making any kind of successful breakthrough against the enemy.

By the end of 1941 many of the battle weary assault gun units, which had taken part in Operation Barbarossa, were no longer fit to fight. Mobile operations had ground to a halt, but fortunately for the exhausted crews and supporting units no mobile operations had been planed during the winter of 1941. In the freezing arctic temperatures a number of the assault guns were pulled out of their stagnant defensive positions in order to rest, reorganize and retrain.

In the meantime, whilst the Eastern Front offered little in the way of a successful military outcome, German designers decided that the development of a long assault gun was needed to meet the growing threat of the Red Army. Initially the gun developed was the 7.5cm cannon 44 L/46. However it was later known as the 7.5cm Panzerjägerkanone 40 L/46, but in mid-March 1942 was renamed the 7.5cm Assault Gun 40 L/43. The L/43 was fitted with the bottle-shaped muzzle brake and the barrel was much more effective at longer ranges.

Up to the end of 1941, the assault guns had all been produced with the short barrel 7.5cm gun. These were the variants Ausf.B, C and D, of which 520 of them had been completed for operations. The Ausf.E came off the production lines in early September 1941 and 275 were transported to the East. By March 1942 the long barrel 7.5cm cannon Ausf.F entered service. It's L/43 armour-piercing Panzergranate 39 shells was designed to be capable of penetrating 91mm of armour plate at a range of 500 metres and was regarded more than sufficient at that time to meet the developing threat of the enemy.

On 1 April 1942, some 623 assault guns were made readily available on the Eastern Front. A month later in May production of the final version of the 7.5cm cannon begun, known as the 7.5cm StuK L/48. Whilst the new gun went into production out on the Eastern Front there was renewed confidence. This begun with the summer offensive, codenamed 'Operation Blau', opening up in southern Russia. Some 15 Panzer divisions and Panzergrenadier divisions of the 1st and 4th Armies, together with Italian, Rumanian and Hungarian formations crashed into action. Supporting the troops were a number of assault guns, and these along with the advancing Panzers made astonishing gains through southern Russia. Although still in relative small numbers the StuG divided its batteries among the individual regiments of a division and were still able to provide effective firepower. However, in spite the success of the assault gun in action during the summer months of 1942, it was hindered was mechanical breakdowns.

A StuG.III Ausf.A advances along a road through France destined for the front lines. This assault gun is indentified as an Ausf.A because it mounts the early idler wheel and the original position of the forward return roller.

A StuG.III negotiates a steep gradient after probably wading through a river. The vehicle is finished in overall dark grey and has a white painted tactical number '24' painted on the side of the vehicles superstructure and on the glacis plate.

Two StuG crew members stand next to a battery of StuGs at a training camp in 1940. It had been in Poland when armoured crews learnt that their vehicles currently in service had demonstrated limitations when fighting took place, especially during close quarter contact. It was for this reason they wanted a vehicle that could show its worth as a fighting vehicle and also provide vital infantry support wherever it was required.

Two photographs showing StuG.III's passing through a French village. The development of this piece of mobile artillery that could fight alongside infantry, as well as keep pace with the lightening advances of *Blitzkrieg*, was an amazing achievement for the *Panzerwaffe* in 1940.

Two StuG.III's moving along a road in the West in 1940. In spite a number of problems with the vehicle prior to the invasion of Russia, the experience in the West showed that the assault gun provided the hard-fighting infantry with valuable support.

An early production model moves through a village. With the vehicles low silhouette for better survivability, it not only provided sterling offensive service, but fought brilliantly during defensive battles as well.

An early variant is parked at the side of a cobbled road. This photograph is more than likely been taken in France. After the battle of France where the StuG had done sterling service orders were immediately given for the production of another 500 machines. These machines equipped the first *Sturmgeschütz* batteries which served in the Blitzkrieg campaigns, through the Balkans and into Russia.

A well camouflaged StuG.III negotiating a steep gradient. Throughout operations in the West, and indeed during the opening offensive in the East in 1941, the StuG remained a very robust, reliable, and effective weapon.

A StuG.III Ausf.B parked at the side of a road beneath some trees during the early part of the invasion of Russia in the summer of 1941. Note the white-painted edge of the rear mud-flap, which was used for low-light driving.

The crew of a StuG.III Ausf.B have halted with their machine during the opening phase of operation 'Barbarossa', the invasion of the Soviet Union in June 1941. During the first weeks of the invasion of Russia, the StuG.III performed very well in an infantry support role.

An StuG.III. Ausf.B hurtles along a dusty round during the summer of 1941 on the Eastern Front. For the invasion of Russia German factories were able to complete 548 StuG.III vehicles. The StuG had a crew of four and came equipped with a 7.5cm StuK 37 L/24 gun capable of traversing from 12.5 degrees left to 12.5 degrees right.

Here a StuG.III Ausf.B passes a damaged bridge, probably during operations in Russia in the summer of 1941. The letter 'B' can just be seen painted on the side of the vehicles superstructure, indicating this was in the second gun battery. Note the crew wearing steel helmets.

A battery of StuG Ausf.B's move along a road supporting infantry. During the summer of 1941 the StuG acquitted itself very well in its first actions in Russia. However, the lack of machine gun for close support against enemy infantry was a problem with early variants.

Two StuG.III's slowly manoeuvre along a road forward of a camouflaged Sd.Kfz.251 halftrack, armed with an MG34 machine gun for local fire support. During the early phase of the invasion of the Soviet Union the StuG proved its worth, especially clearing out enemy infantry in urbanized areas. However, because of its fixed turret it was limited.

A StuG Ausf.C /D with two crew members striding the side of the vehicle hurtle along a dusty round past a recently captured village destined for the front lines. The vehicle always kept pace with the infantry and supported them in almost all roles of engagement, ensuring that massive gains were achieved at all times.

A StuG.III Ausf.B moves along a typical Russia road during the early victories on the Eastern Front. The crew have covered the part of the vehicle with a tarpaulin in order to keep dust out of the gun mantlet.

A battery of StuG.Ausf.C/D move along a track through a field, probably in southern Russia in the summer of 1941. The close formation of the assault guns suggests that the *Luftwaffe* have already secured complete air supremacy in the area.

A group of soldiers have taken cover at the rear of a StuG.III. It appears that the soldiers have spotted enemy aircraft activity. The national flag has been draped over the stowage bins that are attached on the engine deck for aerial recognition.

Opposite: A grenadier is stowing away a flamethrower on the rear of a StuG.III. Throughout the war the StuG was used extensively by grenadiers to be transported from one dangerous front to another.

A StuG.III. Ausf.B, probably at a training barracks in Germany or Poland in 1941. The vehicle displays the tactical number '14' in white on the front glacis of the superstructure. In addition, is the unit's Death's Head insignia painted in yellow beneath the tactical number. This vehicle belonged to the Sturmartillerie-Abteilung 192.

A StuG.III. Ausf.B belonging to the Sturmartillerie-Abteilung 192 motors along a dusty road. Abt.192 saw action on the Eastern Front with the XII-Korps of the 2.Panzer-Group of Army Group Centre.

Two photographs taken in sequence showing a StuG.III has halted beside a road. This Ausf.B variant displays quite nicely its wider 40cm tracks, and by the appearance of mud and grass has undergone some cross-country driving. Note the Notek driving head-lamps mounted on the front of the vehicle. These lights could also be blacked-out.

A StuG.III belonging to the *Sturmartillerie-Abteilung 192* moves at high speed along a dusty road. Although the vehicle is absent of its 'Skull and Crossbones' insignia the tactical number '33' on the casemate positively identifies it belonging to this formation.

An interesting photograph showing a resting crew with their old StuG.III Ausf.A during operations in the Soviet Union in the summer of 1941. Even by this period of the war, there was still a presence of the early variant model StuGs operating effectively in Russia.

The crew of a StuG.III have halted on a dusty road and pose for the camera. The vehicle is painted in overall dark grey and displays the letter 'B' on the side of the vehicles superstructure indicating that it belongs to the 2nd battery.

A StuG.III Ausf.B on the *Ostfront* drives at speed through a village. With the vehicles heavy armour and great off-road capability, the StuG could follow the infantry of the *Panzergruppen* everywhere.

A StuG moving along a typical dusty road somewhere in Russia. The vehicles main task was to suppress heavy infantry and anti-tank weapons that could not be destroyed by heavy infantry weapons.

A StuG.III advances towards the battlefront. As with many of these vehicles because of its unique design there were many leaks and the crew often had to cover the fighting compartment with a specially fitted tarpaulin. Note the vehicles unit marking on the left mud-flap indicating it belongs to the *Sturmartillerie-Abteilung 189*.

An Ausf.B variant has halted on the road with infantrymen on board hitching a lift. Often to maintain the speed of an advance the accompanying infantry were carried into battle on the tanks and other armoured vehicles. When they ran into stiff opposition, they immediately dismounted to avoid taking heavy casualties.

An interesting photograph showing a wounded soldier being transported on board an Ausf.B variant. Note the commander who can be seen behind the scissor periscope, which has been fitted with long tubes to protect the optics from the glare of the sun.

A familiar scene in the Soviet Union during the rapid advances of the German forces in the summer of 1941. An Ausf.B variant can be seen with a national flag draped over the engine deck for aerial recognition, whilst infantry push forward using animal draught and other supporting vehicles.

An Ausf.B variant belonging to the Sturmartillerie-Abteilung 192 moves through a town during an urbanized contact in the summer of 1941. Note the track links attached to the front superstructure of the vehicle for additional armoured protection. By the time the Germans attacked Russia the *Sturmgeschütz* battery strength increased to nine guns.

A StuG.Ausf.C/D moves slowly forward through some undergrowth inside a village. The commander armed with an MP40 machine-gun stands at the ready. As German forces advanced ever deeper in to the Soviet Union they encountered stiffer resistance where StuGs and other armoured vehicles became increasingly embroiled in fighting for each village, town and city.

An early production model negotiates an entrance to a border control. Planning a head for any eventuality, the vehicle can be seen carrying logs on the engine deck; probably to be used if should the weather turn. The vehicle needed to be capable of maintaining mobility especially in boggy and uneven terrain.

An Ausf.B variant advances through a field. This apparent experienced crew has used spare track links to create additional armoured protection to the front of the vehicles superstructure. Behind the StuG is an Sd.Kfz.252 which was a light armoured ammunition transporter for the *Sturmgeschütz* units.

A interesting close-up view of an Ausf.C/D variant that appears to have been experiencing some problems in the boggy terrain. For recovery the crew have also attached their tow cables to the vehicle. This is a typical *Ostfront* scene during the latter half of the summer of 1941, when heavy rain would turn a relatively normal dusty road into a quagmire.

Two StuG Ausf.Bs roll along a dusty road bound for the front lines in the summer of 1941. During the first years on the Eastern Front the assault gun proved indispensible to infantrymen and the elite Waffen-SS alike.

A well camouflaged StuG advances along a road passing a resting column of infantry that have taken cover at the side of the road. Note the MG34 machine gun on its bipod mounting. The advance through the Soviet Union was rapid but by August 1941 there were signs that resistance was increasingly stiffening.

A commander armed with an MP40 sub-machine gun takes cover on a StuG.III and surveyors the battlefield a head through a pair of Zeiss field binoculars. The development of this all purpose built mobile assault gun continued to be successful at supporting the infantry and exacted a deadly toll on enemy armour as well.

An early variant StuG is seen halted on a cobbled road with supporting armour including the Marder and a halftrack towing a 10.5cm field howitzer. These vehicles appear to be on the outskirts of a large town or city. In the distance black smoke rises into the air indicating that there has been some significant aerial activity in the area.

Naked crew members take time-out to wash their vehicle in the heat of the Russian summer during 1941. Throughout the war the *Sturmgeschütz* crews never regarded themselves as tank men. Rather, they were artillerymen manning mobile assault guns.

Foliage has been applied to this StuG.III for additional camouflage protection, especially against the growing might of the Red Army air force that was beginning to cause serious problems by the late summer of 1941. The letter 'A' painted in white on the front of the vehicles superstructure indicated it's the first gun in the battery. Note the unit marking painted on the front of the vehicle.

StuGs bound for the front lines during the summer of 1941. This particular vehicle belongs to the *203. Sturmartillerie-Abteilung* and carries the tactical sign for a self-propelled gun in white. Inside the tactical sign is the designation of the battery, '3/203'. The vehicle number and width markings on the mud-guards are also white.

A StuG.III Ausf.C/D rolling through a village in the height of the summer. Of particular interest is the kill markings painted on the front of the vehicle, which was a rare occurrence on the superstructure. Many units throughout the war painted 'kill' or 'victory' markings on guns or vehicles that had destroyed enemy aircraft, vehicles, or other targets. Victory markings essentially took one or two forms; rings painted on the barrel of the gun, or symbols painted on the shield or superstructure of a weapon.

StuGs churn-up dust as they roll forward along a typical Russian road. Although this assault gun was seen as an offensive weapon, the lack of close-defence weapons and its light side armour meant that it was not very effective in close-quarters fighting.

Ausf.C/D variants advancing along a road, probably in southern Russia. The early variant StuG's continued to be a valuable weapon during the early days of the fighting in Russia in the summer of 1941. Even as late as the summer of 1942 a total of 619 (of the 822 produced) were still active on the Eastern Front.

A StuG.III Ausf.B has just crossed a bridge and is being followed by what appears to be an Sd.kfz.253 ammunition carrier. In the Soviet Union the StuG operated in close support of the infantry, following behind the advancing troops and providing high explosives artillery fire to help overcome any enemy strong points that were holding up the advance.

An early variant StuG appears to have got into some trouble in soft ground and become stuck in overgrowth. Note the unit marking on the side of the vehicles superstructure indicating it belongs to the *Sturmartillerie-Abteilung.191*.

Out in Russia and a StuG crew converse with their commander before resuming operations. Although the StuG proved its worth on the battlefield in 1941, its success would soon diminish as the Red Army began using similar combat vehicles in large numbers.

Here in this photograph infantry are being closely supported by a single StuG.III. Throughout the summer of 1941 this armoured vehicle continued to prove indispensible to infantrymen and the elite formations of the *Waffen-SS*.

A StuG.III Ausf.B crossing is crossing a river during operations in the summer of 1941. It clearly shows the vehicles kill rings painted in white on the short-barreled 7.5cm gun. The photo also gives a very good view of the tapering 'trench' left of the gun mantlet, which led back to the gunner's frontal sight aperture.

A unique interior view of a knocked out early variant StuG somewhere in Russia. By the look of the vehicle there has been extensive fire damage.

An Ausf.B variant has halted in a field with a number of other components accompanying the battery to the front lines. A 1-ton Sd.Kfz.10 carrying StuK rounds of ammunition is parked next the StuG, obviously being used to re-supply the vehicle for its onward journey.

A rear shot of a StuG.III.Ausf.C/D as it climbs a small gradient in the road to join the vehicle column. As with many armoured vehicles in the late summer of 1941, many crews used spare track lengths and spare road wheels to create additional armoured protection.

Two StuG crewmen stand next to their stranded assault gun. Due the weight of the vehicle it has apparently slipped into the water and lies at an angle. Many experienced crews attached their tow cables to the receptacles on the rear hull plate in order to shorten the time for recovery. Note that the crew members have been removing items from the rear of the engine deck including the spare road wheels. This was obviously done to lighten the load and make recovery easier.

An early variant StuG moves along a road. The vehicle has received two track links attached to the front of the superstructure in a drastic attempt to mitigate against penetration of the thin armour by Russian infantry anti-tank rifles.

A StuG.III Ausf.C/D motors along a road. A soldier can just be seen perched on top of the vehicle armed with an MG34 for local defence. One of the biggest drawbacks that StuG crews encountered on the Eastern Front was the lack of local defence. As the war dragged on it soon became imperative that the vehicle would have to be defended by machine gun.

A somber photograph showing an infantryman standing next to a grave. Parked nearby beneath some trees is a StuG.III. Ausf.B.

An interesting photograph showing a recovered StuG being transported by rail on a specially adapted flat railcar in the early winter of 1941. The broken track link indicates that the vehicle has obviously been damaged by enemy fire, and is being moved to one of the Sturmgeschütz workshops in the rear. Note the Sd.Kfz.9 being utilized as a locomotive to pull the flat car.

A StuG has halted in the snow and infantry including a motorcyclist can be seen standing next to the machine. Even with the high losses of the Sturmgeschütz on the Eastern Front the crews still had high regard for their self-propelled assault guns as a decisive weapon of war.

An early StuG is parked in the snow with two of the crew members in the vehicles compartment. Throughout the summer of 1941 official regulations had stressed that the StuG should be employed in the Soviet Union en masse. However, by the winter of 1941 the constant demands of the war meant that they were often being employed as single battalions or even single machines. This consequently led to high losses of StuGs in the first year of fighting on the Eastern Front.

A StuG negotiates through a rubble strewn town following bitter fighting somewhere on the Eastern Front. The vehicles were used primarily to neutralize enemy support weapons at short ranges over open sights, and to always co-operate with infantry to penetrate and breakthrough enemy lines. This was also undertaken during urbanized contacts too.

Chapter Two

Ost Front
1942-1943

During the late summer and early autumn of 1942 *Sturmgeschütz* units once more proved themselves on the battlefield. The long barreled L/43 gun gave the crews better armour piercing capability and therefore greater tank killing capacity than ever before. However, every crew member was totally aware of the real disadvantages of no turret but soon learned to adopt defensive tactics that were designed to lure Soviet armour into carefully planned killing grounds.

These new tactics were employed all over the Eastern Front and especially during the second winter where in many areas the front stagnated.

In order to take advantage of their new tactics and increase the potential tank killing capability of the StuG in late 1942, the Ausf.G variant assault gun was produced. The vehicle was armed with a powerful 7.5cm Assault Canon 40 L/48. The Ausf.G chassis had a wider body with a commander's cupola. The commander's field of view was massively enhanced and allowed the crew to quickly locate areas of ground to suitably take cover or seek-out enemy movement. Along with these modifications the vehicles superstructure's armour thickness was increased in the frontal area. On the StuG.III.Ausf.F and F/8 for instance, which was produced in 1942, the front armour plates had already been thickened to 80mm.

During the early summer of 1943, the first assault gun hulls were produced with 80mm bow armour. Pz.Kpfw.III hulls were also used, but were fitted with heavier armour. This heavier armour and longer gun barrel made the newer StuG.III variants some 2-tons heavier than those assault guns that entered the Soviet Union a year earlier. Although the Red Army found that these new generation variants more potent and harder to knock-out the crews found that because of their weight it decreased mobility.

However, in spite its weight the Ausf.G was well armoured which subsequently gave it a strong defensive capability without it losing its ability to make counterthrusts. But instead of it being a weapon for primarily supporting the infantry, it had become yet another defensive weapon with its main task of killing tanks. Yet, it could still be used in an offensive actions as well, which was seen extensively in early July 1943.

A white-washed StuG.III has become imbedded in the thick snow and the crew of a Pz.Kpfw.III are attempting to pull the assault gun out by using tow cables. The first winter on the Eastern Front was punishing for both infantry and the *Panzerwaffe*. The harsh temperatures led to many armoured vehicles breaking down or becoming immovable in the arctic weather. The consequences of this led to the German front grounding to a halt and being overrun in a number of areas by well adapted Soviet forces.

In June 1943, 21 Panzer divisions, including four *Waffen-SS* divisions and two Panzergrenadier divisions were being prepared for a large scale armoured attack called Operation *Zitadelle* in the Kursk salient. For this massive attack the *Panzerwaffe* were able to muster in early July 17 divisions and two brigades with no less than 1,715 Panzers and 147 StuG.III assault guns. Each division averaged some 98 Panzers and self-propelled anti-tank guns.

Putting together such a strong force was a great achievement, but the Panzerwaffe of 1943 were unlike those armoured forces that had victoriously steamrolled across western Russia two years earlier. The losses during the previous winter had resulted in the drastic

A column of whitewashed StuG.III's during the early winter of 1942 on the Eastern Front. Even in harsh winter weather German policy still outlined that all times assault guns were to advance with or just behind the infantry. They were never to go ahead of the infantry, and when an objective was reached the assault gun was to remain with the infantry whilst the position was being consolidated, but retire about 1000 yards to await further assignment.

reductions in troop strength. Despite the Panzerwaffe's impressive array of firepower, this shortage of infantry was to lead to Panzer units being required to take on more ambitious tasks normally preserved for the infantry. The Panzerwaffe was determined to rejuvenate their Blitzkrieg tactics, but the immense preparations that had gone into constructing the Soviet defences meant that the Panzerwaffe were never ever going to succeed penetrating into the strategic depths of the Red Army fortifications with any overriding success.

When the attack was finally unleashed in the pre-dawn light of 5 July 1943, the Germans were stunned by the dogged defence of their Red foe. The battle was unlike any other engagement they had previously encountered. Within two weeks of the battle many of the assault guns came to grief by well sighted enemy anti-tank defences. In a number of areas

A crewman flexes his muscles whilst conversing with his comrades, while they all gather around a StuG.III.Ausf.B. All the crew wears the now familiar assault gun uniform which was similar cut to that of their *Panzertruppen* counterparts.

the infantry, which were otherwise supported by the StuG, were overpowered by strong defensive positions.

The losses that the Panzerwaffe sustained at Kursk were so immense that it undoubtedly led to the German Army taking their first steps of its slow retreat back towards Germany. The Russians had managed to destroy no less than 30 divisions, seven of which were Panzer. German reinforcements were insufficient to replace the staggering losses, so they fought on under-strength.

The reverberations caused by the Defeat at Kursk meant that German forces in the south bore the brunt of the heaviest Soviet drive. Both the Russian Voronezh and Steppe Fronts possessed massive local superiority against everything the Germans had on the battlefield, and this included their diminishing resources of tanks and assault guns. The Panzerwaffe were now duty-bound to improvise with what they had at their disposal and try to maintain themselves in the field, and in doing so they hoped to wear the enemy's offensive capacity. But in the south where the weight of the Soviet effort was directed, Army Group South's line began breaking and threatened to be ripped wide open. Stiff defensive action was now the stratagem placed upon the Panzerwaffe, but they lacked sufficient reinforcements and the strength of their armoured units dwindled steadily as they tried to hold back the Russian might.

Two StuGs heavily laden with supplies festooned to the engine deck have halted in a field during a short break in their relentless drive during the early spring of 1942. A halftrack more than likely bringing up ammunition for the StuG crew has pulled alongside one of the assault guns. Infantry with animal draught can also be seen along with other support vehicles.

A smiling crewman poses for the camera next to his StuG.III Ausf.B. The photographs gives an excellent close-up view of the vehicles idler wheel and stowage gear onboard the engine deck. Note the two traffic signal sticks protruding out of the stowed wheel, partly covered by the tarpaulin.

A StuG.III moves forward along a road with a large stowage bin attached to the engine deck. The vehicle would have been carrying a varied quality of high explosives, smoke and armour piercing rounds and supplies for the crew in order to sustain them on their ever increasing long journey eastwards.

An excellent view of a battery of assault guns including a long column of Ausf.B variants and the newly introduced StuG.III Ausf.F leading the advance. The Ausf F was armed with the 7.5cm StuK40 L/43. The new gun was over a metre longer than the StuK37 L/24 used on the StuG III Ausf C/D, giving it a higher muzzle velocity, and thus a better armour piercing capability. During the production run of the Ausf F received 30mm armour plates welded onto the front of the hull and superstructure, starting with the last eleven machines produced in June 1942, and continuing on for the last 182 machines. Two headlights on the upper hull front were also removed.

A crewman of a 1-ton Sd.Kfz.10 hands a StuK round to his comrade in the loaders hatch of a StuG.III.Ausf.B. Note the national flag attached to the front of the halftrack for aerial recognition purposes. By mid-1942 such activities were eventually phased out by crews as they found that the Red Army air force could easily target-in on the vehicles.

Infantry have hitched a lift onboard a StuG.III.Ausf.F. The vehicle displays two antennae, which indicates that it is a command vehicle. The assault gun is indentified as a Ausf.F due to the long StuK40 L/48, but without the muzzle brake.

Another photograph of a crewman handing StuK ammunition to an assault gun crew from a halftrack. Re-supplying these vehicles was vital for the continuation of the war effort, especially against the growing might of the Soviet Army.

A StuG.III.Ausf.F has been secured ready for transport on a railway flatcar during the summer of 1942. It appears that the vehicle has been choked but not secured for transport. One of the crewman can be seen posing with his vehicle partly wearing his uniform.

Two Ausf.F variants have halted along a road. Parked nearby is a Pz.Kpfw.III. During the first months on the Eastern Front it was soon recognized that the StuG.III needed to be up-gunned in order to compete against the growing might of the Red Army. In March of 1942, the Ausf F entered production and was finally introduced on the battlefield weeks later. Out in the Soviet Union it was regarded not only an assault gun, but also a badly needed tank destroyer.

A StuG.III Ausf.F moves along a road most probably on the outskirts of Stalingrad in the late summer of 1942. The vehicle is fitted with the new StuK40 long-gun barrel, and the double-baffle muzzle brake. Note the track links bolted to the rear of the superstructure plate.

An Ausf.B variant moving along a sandy road somewhere in the Russian heartlands during the summer of 1942. By this period of the war more and more German armour was being up-gunned to meet the ever increasing threat of the growing might of the Soviet Army.

An Ausf.F variant halts somewhere on the Russian steppe. An unarmed captured Soviet soldier can be seen approaching the vehicle. The national cross insignia painted in black with a white outline is seen on the pannier side of the StuG.

A light armoured ammunition transporter for StuG units crosses a small river. These vehicles were issued to the *Sturmgeschütz* units. One vehicle carried ammunition (Sd.Kfz.252), whilst the other was a battery command observation vehicle (Sd.Kfz.253).

A Sd.kfz 252 belonging to an unidentified *Sturmgeschütz* unit is parked at what appears to be a training barracks. This vehicle was powered by a Maybach HL42 TRKM 6-cyclinder petrol engine that developed 100 horsepower at 2800 RPM, which drove the vehicle to a maximum speed of 40 mph on the road. The base vehicle weighed 6.4-tons, was 15-feet long, 6.3-feet wide, and 5.2-feet high.

A decorated assault gun crewmember posing for the camera. This special field-grey uniform was worn by all crews of tank destroyer and self-propelled assault gun units. The style of the uniform was very similar to that of the black Panzer uniform, but this special garment was made entirely of field-grey cloth. The collar patches too differed by those crews of different types of military units that were entitled to wear the uniform.

A StuG.III.Ausf.F parked at a barracks next to a whitewashed Pz.Kpfw.IV during the autumn of 1942. By 1 April 1942, there were some 623 StuGIII's available on the Eastern Front. These figures were soon to rise dramatically.

Crewmembers of a whitewashed Ausf.F have halted next to a building. An Sd.Kfz.252 halftrack has pulled alongside the StuG and one of the crew is handing fresh supplies of StuK40 ammunition through the vehicles hatch.

General Heinz Guderian can be seen conferring with a StuG.III Ausf.F crew in the winter of 1942. The vehicle has received a complete winter whitewash. Note the protective covering over the 7.5cm StuK40 muzzle break.

A new whitewashed StuG.III Ausf.G variant in a field. This was the final variant to be manufactured, and it came off the production line in 1943, and was rushed straight into service. The Ausf.G was armed with an MG34 for local defence and featured periscope to give the commander some protection as he surveyed the local terrain.

A battery of whitewashed StuGs with supporting halftracks during the winter of 1943. They have halted inside a town to afford some kind of concealment from aerial detection. The crews wear an assortment of winter clothing and headgear including the winter reversible jacket.

A StuG crewmember stands proudly next to his Ausf.F machine somewhere on the Eastern Front. The *Panzerjäger Obergefreiter* wears the special field-grey uniform of the tank destroyer and self-propelled assault gun units. The garment was a very practical piece of clothing, and unlike the black Panzer uniform, it was less conspicuous when the crewmen left his vehicle.

A StuG.III Ausf.G belonging to an unidentified *Waffen-SS* unit is towing a four wheeled vehicle over muddy terrain. Note the installed MG34 machine gun with splinter shield. Four SS grenadiers have hitched a lift onboard the vehicle.

What appears to be a StuG.III Ausf.G moving along a road creating a large dust cloud as it advances towards the front. By early 1943 the StuG had become a very popular assault gun, especially on the Eastern Front. Its low profile and mechanical reliability saw their employment grow on the battlefield. Some 3,041 of them were operational in 1943 alone.

An Sd.Kfz.252 munitions halftrack is seen parked next to a StuG.III.Ausf.G in 1943. The vehicle has an application of Zimmerit anti-magnetic mine paste. Logs have been festooned to this assault gun in order to help it negotiate some of the boggy local terrain.

A StuG.III.Ausf.G crew, possibly in Italy in 1943, has halted during a road march. Note the vehicles armoured side skirts lying on the engine deck whilst the crew undertake some maintenance.

Opposite: One of the most common and practical methods of transporting armour was by rail. Here a Sturmgeschütz unit is being readied for transportation most probably to the Eastern Front. Note the smoke candle dischargers attached to the side of the vehicles superstructure.

Three StuGs can be seen operating in an open field during the early summer of 1943. The assault gun in the middle is an Ausf.F/8 variant, whilst the other two are standard Ausf.F models. The Ausf.F series was the first StuG to be introduced with the longer L/43 calibre StuK40, and then the L/48 calibre weapon.

The crew converse with their commander onboard a halted StuG.III Ausf.G in the late summer of 1943. From 1943 until the end of the war the assault guns were slowly absorbed into the Panzer units, Panzer, and Panzergrenadier divisions of the *Wehrmacht* and *Waffen-SS*.

Two Ausf.G's halted on a muddy road. The StuG crews are using the forest as concealment against both aerial and ground observation. The longer barreled cannon and the modification of the frontal superstructure increased the overall weight of the vehicle to 21.3-tons.

An Ausf.G in an open field. Foliage has been applied liberally to this vehicle, but due to its camouflaged colour scheme it still blends well with the local terrain. By this period of the war losses of tracked vehicles through aerial attack had mounted significantly.

A StuG advances at speed along a typical Soviet road. By 1943 the *Panzerwaffe* were increasingly hard-pressed as the Soviet war machine was applying newer technology to compete against the German assault guns.

A battery of *Sturmgeschütz* is seen advancing in the open following a long twisting road. Note how these Ausf.G's are purposely spaced-apart to reduce the possibility of an airstrike. Russian airpower was the most dangerous opponent armoured crews faced. By late 1943 the Soviet air force dominated many areas in Russia causing extensive damage on the assault guns.

Two photographs taken in sequence showing StuG's halted in a field with their crews conversing next to one of the assault guns. The long distances in which the crews travelled were grueling and a welcome break was almost always greeted with relief.

Two photographs showing a battery of StuGs on special flat-bed railway cars destined for the front. In typical German fashion these vehicles have been chocked and prepared for transportation. All retaining chains and cables are secured and in place.

The crew of a Ausf.F have halted in a field during a pause in operations somewhere on the Eastern Front. Note the tarpaulin fitted around the welded gun mantle and the casemate roof. This was done in order to keep the assault gun dry from the elements.

An Ausf.G is guided onto a flatbed railcar by the man in the foreground. Zimmerit anti-magnetic mine paste has been applied to the vehicles superstructure. As with all StuGs being transported by rail tarpaulin was always attached over the vehicle to protect it from the elements.

Two photographs showing the frontal view of a StuG.III.Ausf.G whilst operating on the Eastern Front. Though the Germans required more assault guns to combat the growing menace of the Red Army production of the Ausf.G was initially curtailed due to heavy allied air raids on the factories. However, in spite the problems, many Ausf G variants were still to appear on the *Ost front* as formidable weapons of war and helped hinder the enemy the best they could.

An interesting photograph showing some of the early production models of the Ausf.G type in the winter of 1943. All these vehicles have received an application of winter white wash with winter tracks. These vehicles are probably from the famous SS-Division 'Das Reich' in the Kharkov area.

A nice image showing two whitewashed StuG.III's in the depths of a Russian winter. Both vehicles have received an application of winter whitewash paint and have just entered a village. Note the large stowage bins attached to the rear of the engine deck.

Chapter Three

On the Defensive
1943-1944

Along the entire Eastern Front the situation was dire. In Army Group Centre and Army Group North German forces were trying desperately to hold the Soviets back from breaking through their lines. Replacements continued to trickle through to help bolster the under strength Panzerwaffe. But in truth, the average new assault gunner that was freshly recruited was not as well trained as his predecessors during the early part of the campaign in Russia. Nevertheless, as with many StuG men they were characterized by high morale and a determination to do their duty.

In almost three months since the defeat at Kursk Army Centre and South had been pushed back an average distance of 150 miles on a 650 mile front. Despite heavy resistance in many sectors of the front the Soviets lost no time in exploiting the fruits of regaining as much territory as possible.

As the winter of 1943 approached there was a further feeling of despair and disbelief that the war had turned against the Germans. During this period there was an exasperating series of deliberations for the Panzerwaffe. Much of its concerns were preventing the awesome might of the Red Army with what little they had available at their disposal. Yet, the quality of the German infantry in late 1943 was no longer comparable to that at the beginning of the Russian campaign in June 1941.

Whilst drastic measures were made to ensure that infantry defended their lines the assault gun forces were still being frantically increased to help counter the massive set-backs. In 1943 some fifty-five percent of the Panzerwaffe comprised of assault guns. They were now found in numerous units. The divisions and brigades of the *Waffen-SS* which even had their own battery or even an entire unit. There were also a number of *Luftwaffe* divisions that had their own assault gun units like the famous Herman Goring Panzer-Korps. In the *Wehrmacht* for instance there were divisions with their own assault gun unit or battery. By the beginning of September 1943, *Panzerjäger* units of the various divisions also received their own assault gun units. This was undertaken in order to compensate for the lack of tanks and many of the Panzer and Panzergrenadier divisions began absorbing many of the artillery assault gun units into the Panzer troops. However, although the assault guns continued to prove their worth within these units, equipping some of the Panzer units with assault guns did not operate well alongside the tank. Although commanders were well aware of the situation, they knew they had no choice. Instead, they continued using assault guns extensively in the Panzer units until the end of the war.

During this period they pushed the StuG further and deeper into the combat zone as an effective tank killer. In late 1943 and early 1944 the assault guns were increasingly equipping the Panzerjäger companies. The StuG continued to fight very effectively, in spite the overwhelming resistance of the enemy. In many areas the front could not be held for any appreciable time and a slow withdrawal ensued much to the anger of Hitler.

Throughout January and February 1944 the winter did nothing to impede the Soviet might from grinding further west. During February the organization of an assault gun battery was changed consisting of four platoons, one of which had three 10.5cm assault howitzer 42 units. Three platoons each equipped with three 7.5cm assault cannon 40 units. Together with two assault guns of the battery leader, there were fourteen vehicles in each battery.

The alteration was supposed to make the gun batteries more effective on the battlefield. Whilst it increased the fire power crews still found they were numerically outnumbered and as a direct consequence still suffered heavy losses.

Yet, despite the setbacks, by the time the spring thaw arrived in March and early April 1944, there was a genuine feeling of motivation within the ranks of the assault gun units. There was renewed determination to keep the Red Army out of the Homeland. In addition, confidence was further bolstered by the efforts of the armaments industry as they begun producing many new vehicles for the Eastern Front. In fact during 1944 the Panzerwaffe were better supplied with equipment during any other time on the Eastern Front, thanks to the armaments industry. In total some 20,000 fighting vehicles including 8,328 medium and heavy tanks, 5,751 assault guns, 3,617 tank destroyers and 1,246 self-propelled artillery carriages of various types reached the Eastern Front. Included in these new arrivals were the second generation of tank-destroyers, the Jagdpanzer IV, followed by the Hetzer and then the Jagpanther and Jagdtiger. In fact, tank-destroyers and assault guns now outnumbered the tanks, which was confirmation of the Panzerwaffe's obligation to performing a defensive role against overwhelming opposition. All of these vehicles would have to be irrevocably stretched along a very thin Eastern Front, with many of them rarely reaching the proper operating level.

Two photographs taken in sequence showing a late variant StuG.III.Ausf.G laden with grenadiers during the late winter of 1943. In order to maintain their speed, the accompanying infantry were carried into battle on assault guns and other armoured vehicles. When they ran into stiff opposition, they immediately dismounted to avoid taking heavy casualties.

Infantry stand beside a muddy road watching a passing column of armoured vehicles. A whitewashed StuG.III leads the drive. Many of the roads in which the armoured vehicles had to follow were often like a quagmire that frequently brought a rapid drive to a crawl, hindering operations in the East.

A whitewashed StuG.III Ausf.G in the depths of a the Russian winter in late 1943. To the right of the crewman the vehicles MG34 machine gun for local defence can be seen mounted behind the splinter shield.

The crew of a white washed Ausf.G variant pose for the camera during a lull in the fighting in the late winter of 1944. Throughout the mid war years the assault gun provided crucial mobile fire support to the infantry, and it also proved its worth as an invaluable anti-tank vehicle.

Two StuG.III Ausf.G's halted inside what appears to be a decimated village somewhere on the Ost front. The leading assault gun has missing side skirting armour plates' indicating that it has been embroiled in some heavy enemy contact.

Three photographs showing grenadiers hitching a lift on board Ausf.G variant assault guns during winter defensive operations in early 1944. Panzergrenadiers were considered elite frontline units and were known for their elite frontline mobility. Often they would advance into battle with assault guns and other armoured vehicles, which offered them armour protection and mobility until they were close enough to attack enemy positions on foot.

A blurred photograph showing an assault gun crew posing in front of their vehicle during a halt in defensive operations on the Eastern Front in early 1944. In spite the StuG's proven tank-killing potential and its service on the battlefield both in offensive and defensive roles, the increased use of the StuG as a anti-tank weapon began depriving the infantry of the fire support for which the assault gun was originally built.

An excellent view of a battery of whitewashed Ausf.G variants in a field during operations on the Eastern Front in the early winter of 1944. Two of the vehicles have missing armoured side skirt plates, more than likely ripped off during heavy sustained enemy contact. The assault gun leading the drive still retains its side armour.

A StuG.III.Ausf.G with intact armoured plating side-skirting is embroiled in action against an enemy target during defensive operations on the Eastern Front during the early winter of 1944. By early 1944, the military situation in Russia was dire for the German Army. It had entered into the New Year with a dwindling number of soldiers to man the battle lines. The Red Army, however, was now even greater in strength than ever before and Hitler's reluctance to concede territory was still proving to be very problematic.

A staff car pulls alongside a StuG.III.Ausf.G. The vehicle carries the square pennant associated with that of a divisional commander, and a triangle-shaped pennant of an Armee or Armee-Gruppe commander.

Three crewmembers with their whitewashed StuG.III.Ausf.F/8 in late 1943 or early 1944 on the Eastern Front. Of interest, note the wire anti-grenade cage over the gunners Sfl.Z.F. 1a sight opening and the cast cover visible over the engine deck hatch lid.

An Ausf.G variant out on a vast Russian plain during operations in the Soviet Union in the early winter of 1944. In January 1944, Hitler had prohibited all voluntary withdrawals and reserved all decisions for himself. This subsequently put more pressure on the *Panzerwaffe* to hold the crumbling lines, and as a direct result saw massive losses of armour trying in vain to support the overwhelmed infantry.

An assault gun crew poses in front of their StuG in the late winter of 1943. The vehicle has not received any application of winter whitewash paint, but the crew has attempted to crudely camouflage it with branches from a tree.

A StuG.III well concealed in undergrowth. The crew are preparing the StuG for action during operations in 1943.

A StuG.III.Ausf.G in undergrowth. This vehicle displays a factory camouflage scheme of red brown or olive green with small stripes of dark yellow. The vehicle has been fitted with a folding shield for the loaders MG34.

An excellent photograph showing StuG.III.Ausf.F/8s forming part of a load destined for Poland in the spring or summer of 1944. These vehicles are part of the famous Herman Goring Panzer-Korps that saw defensive action in Poland in the late summer of 1944. Note all the cast covers over the engine decks access hatch lids to protect the machine from the elements.

Two photographs showing officers inspecting a unit from the Herman Goring division as it simulates battle conditions prior to deployment with Army Group Vistula in October 1944. The Fallschirmjager-Panzer-Korps Herman Goring was activated in early October 1944, and the Herman Goring Panzer-Division, along with its sister Panzergrenadier division, was transferred to the command of the corps.

Two photographs showing Luftwaffe troops belonging to the Herman Goring Division in Poland during the summer of 1944, with a StuG.III.Ausf.F/8. The Herman Goring Division fought hard on the Eastern Front and as a result sustained huge casualties.

Two photographs showing a StuG.III.Ausf.G with very interesting camouflage paint. The armoured side skirt plates have been painted in a pattern of green and brown over the dark yellow sand base. Dense groups of small dots and curving streaks have also been applied. Note the factory built stowage bin attached on the rear of the engine deck.

What appears to be a StuG.III.Ausf.G attached to a Waffen-SS unit. The assault gun has an interesting summer camouflage scheme of dark yellow base with bands of olive green. Note half of the armoured skirting which is missing following a contact with an enemy anti-tank shell.

Support troops are photographed next to a whitewashed ammunition carrier during winter operation on the Eastern Front in early 1944. One man is servicing the vehicle. This vehicle is armed with an MG34 with splinter shield.

An interesting image captured the moment a StuG.III.Ausf.G becomes embroiled in a fire fight with the enemy somewhere on the Eastern Front. Infantry can be seen onboard the vehicle trying to take evasive cover behind the machine guns splinter shield.

Summer 1944 and an Ausf.G variant have halted along a dirt track. The crew is seen conversing with other assault gun crews that have also stopped along the track. Note how the vehicle has purposely moved close to the forest off the track in order to help conceal it from aerial detection. Foliage too has been applied to the superstructure in order to help break up its distinctive shape and prevent it being discovered from the air by Soviet fighters that had by this stage of the war total control of the skies.

Soviet troops surveyor a knocked out StuG.III.Ausf.G. The vehicles side skirts have been blown off by enemy anti-tank fire, probably in a previous contact. Note the spare track links on the hull side plates for additional armoured protection. Whilst the track links afforded some protection they were no match against armour piercing shots that could penetrate deeper than 30mm-thick.

A column of StuG.III.Ausf.G's laden with Panzergrenadiers in Poland in September or early October 1944. The Panzergrenadiers would frequently accompany the armoured spearhead, mounted on board the assault guns in the first wave, followed immediately by a second wave of Panzergrenadiers in armoured halftracks who would overcome the enemy positions that had survived the first wave.

In order to anticipate becoming stuck along the muddy roads the crew of these two StuG.III.Ausf.G's have readied their tow cables. Driving throughout the Soviet Union, and indeed in Poland as well, could be tremendously hazardous. A sudden down pour could reduce an otherwise normal uneven road into a muddy swamp.

A Waffen-SS grenadier belonging to the premier 5.*Waffen-SS* Panzer-Division '*Wiking*' surveyors the terrain standing next to a stationary StuG.III.Ausf.F/8 in the summer of 1944.

A late version StuG.III. Ausf.G advancing along a road probably on the Western Front in 1944. From 1943 until the end of the war the assault guns were slowly absorbed into the Panzer units, Panzer and Panzer grenadier divisions of the *Wehrmacht* and *Waffen-SS*.

A late variant StuG.III.Ausf.G passes the photographer heading towards the battle front. By the appearance of the crew wearing tropical uniforms it is more than likely that his photograph was taken in northern Italy in the summer of 1944.

A StuG.III.Ausf.G on a road in early winter of 1944. Tarpaulin is protecting the vehicle from the harsh weather. By 1944 because of the lack of tanks in the dwindling ranks of the Panzer divisions, the StuG.III was used alongside the Panzer until the end of the war. However, in spite the numerous advantages of the assault guns, equipping the Panzer units with these vehicles did not blend well with the nature of the Panzer.

The crew pose for the camera on their early production StuG.III.Ausf.G. Note how the crew have fitted the a rack of spare tracks on the vehicles casemate side wall.

A camouflaged StuG.III.Ausf.G with intact side-skirts can just be seen with some foliage attached. The vehicle is probably attached to a Bulgarian unit during anti-partisan operations. The Bulgarian StuG was known as the Maybach T-III.

A well camouflaged StuG.III more than likely operating in Italy. Note the smoke candle dischargers attached to the side of the vehicles superstructure.

An excellent photo of a 7.5cm gun barrel of an unidentified StuG.III out on the Russian steep. Despite the longer 7.5cm barrel this assault gun was continually hard pressed on the battlefield and constantly called upon for offensive and defensive fire support, where it was gradually compelled to operate increasingly in an anti-tank roll.

A StuG.III.Ausf.G has halted in what appears to be a orchard during operations in northern Italy in 1944. Note the distinctive commander's cupola. Also of interest is the tarpaulin protecting the mantle of the gun.

This page and opposite: Five photographs showing assault gun men. Apart from the uniforms worn by the Panzer crews, a special uniform was introduced for both *Sturmartillerie* and *Panzerjäger* units. The uniform was specially designed primarily to be worn inside and away from their armoured vehicles, and for this reason designers had produced a garment that gave better camouflage qualities than the standard black Panzer uniform. The uniform worn by units of the *Panzerjäger* was made entirely from lightweight grey-green wool material. The cut was very similar to that of the black Panzer uniform. However, it did differ in respect of insignia and the collar patches.

An assault gun prowling a Soviet town. By the appearance of the protected muzzle break the vehicle has not been involved in any urbanized confrontation. The unit marking of an elephant painted on the side the superstructure indicates that it belongs to the StuG.Brigade.203.

A support vehicle is resupplying a StuG.IV with 7.5cm StuK ammunition. In spite the German military reversal on the Eastern Front the Panzerwaffe would extensively use the assault gun in a number of prominent roles in both major offensive and defensive employments.

A StuG.III. inside a decimated town in the summer of 1944. Despite dogged resistance in the south assault gun units lacking reinforcements began to steadily dwindle. As further losses multiplied, armour which had not been destroyed or encircled was forced to withdraw.

A number of StuG.III.Ausf.G's are seen here taking cover in a dip in the terrain during Operation Bargration in July 1944. Bagration – the Russian code-name for the 1944 summer offensive, led to the destruction of Army Group Centre. The offensive cost the Wehrmacht more men and material than the catastrophe at Stalingrad sixteen months earlier. This shattering defeat of Army Group Centre saw the loss of over 300,000 men and resulted in Soviet forces pushing back exhausted German remnants out of Russia through Poland to the gates of Warsaw.

Two soldiers move forward supported by a StuG.III.Ausf.G with intact side skirts during Operation Bagration. By 4 July 1944, the military situation of Army Group Centre was calamitous and it was fast becoming clear how rapidly their armoured force was diminishing. The absence of communications too made it impossible for assault gun crew for instance to access the full extent of disintegration. There seemed no stopping the tide of the Russian advance, and as they remorselessly pushed forward *Sturmgeschütz* units became increasingly confused and entangled in bitter bloody fighting.

An assault gun can be seen moving at speed across open ground. By mid-1944 hard pressed battles were fought all over the Eastern Front. Despite the fact that new defensive lines were constructed troop strength and the lack of weapons were so depleted that nothing could be done to avert many units becoming encircled and then annihilated.

An assault gun crew rest during a pause in the fighting with their Ausf.G. A halftrack command vehicle can be seen parked nearby. By mid-1944 shortages in men and equipment had worsened considerably causing many problems for the assault gun crews deployed in both offensive and defensive roles.

Chapter Four

The Demise of the
Sturmgeschütz
1944-1945

By the spring of 1944 there was yet again a feeling of renewed confidence in the East. But by the summer as news reached the forward units that the Allies had landed on the northern shores of France on 6 June 1944, deep concerns began to fester on how they would be able to distribute their forces between two fronts. The problems became far greater during the third week of June when a new summer offensive by the Russians called 'Operation Bagration' was launched with its sole objective to annihilate Army Group Centre. Opposing the massive Russian force was three German armies with thirty-seven divisions, weakly supported by armour, against 166 divisions, supported by 2,700 tanks and 1,300 assault guns.

By the end of the first week of Bagration the three German armies had lost between them nearly 200,000 men and 900 tanks and assault guns; 9th Army and the 3rd Panzer Army were almost decimated. The remnants of the shattered armies trudged back west in order to try and rest and refit what was left of its Panzer units and build new defensive lines. Any plans to regain the initiative on the Eastern Front were doomed forever.

Although German commanders were fully aware of the fruitless attempts by its forces to establish a defensive line, Panzer and assault gun units followed instructions implicitly in a number of areas to halt the Soviet drive. Again and again the units fought to the grim death. Despite the huge losses and lack of reserves many still remained resolute stemming the Soviet drive east, even if it meant giving ground and fighting in Poland, which was regarded as the last defensive position before Germany.

During the summer of 1944 the Germans began defending Poland against the Soviet might. By September 1944, the whole position in Poland was on the point of disintegration. Action in Poland had been a grueling battle of attrition for those German units that had managed to escape from the slaughter. Fortunately for the surviving German forces, the

Soviet offensive had now run out of momentum. The Red Army's troops were too exhausted, and their armoured vehicles were in great need of maintenance and repair. It seemed the Germans were spared from being driven out of Poland for the time being.

By late 1944 it became increasingly obvious that the assault gun, although built in huge numbers, were no longer as effective on the battlefield. Whilst the 7.5cm 40 L/40 gun was still regarded as a lethal weapon, the Russians had already developed newer and larger anti-tank killers of their own with greater armoured protection and better fire power. As a result the Russians continued pushing forward.

On 12 January 1945, the Eastern Front erupted with a massive advance as the 1st Ukrainian Front made deep wide-sweeping penetrations against hard-pressed German formations. The Russian offensive was delivered with so much weight and fury never before experienced on the Eastern Front. Two days later on 14 January, the 1st Belorrussian Front began its long awaited drive along the Warsaw-Berlin axis, striking out from the Vistula south of Warsaw. The city was quickly encircled and fell three days later. The frozen ground ensured rapid movement for the Russian tank crews, but in some areas these massive advances were halted for a time by the skilful dispositions of Panzer and Panzerjäger units. By this time the action strength of the Sturmgeschütz units had fallen to an all time low. Losses of equipment too had increased markedly in the course of the retreat combat. Often assault gun crews would abandon their vehicles when they ran out of fuel and were seen regularly running on foot or hitching a lift onboard other StuG vehicles.

In early 1945, production figures dropped, and as a result of this decline units no longer had any reserves on which to rely on. When defensive fighting began in Germany there was a severe lack of fuel, spare parts, and the lack of trained crews. When parts of the front caved the remaining assault gun units were often forced to destroy their equipment, so nothing was left for the conquering enemy. The Germans no longer had the manpower, war plant or transportation to accomplish a proper build-up of forces on the Oder. Commanders could do little to compensate for the deficiencies, and in many sectors of the front they did not have any coherent planning in the event of any defensive position being lost.

During the last days of the war most of the remaining assault guns continued to fight as a unit until they destroyed their equipment and surrendered. At the time of surrender, the combined strength of the entire Panzerwaffe was 2,023 tanks, 738 assault guns and 159 Flakpanzers. Surprisingly this was the same strength that was used to attack Russia in 1941. But the size of German Army in 1945 was not the same; it was far too inadequate in strength for any type of task. Although the war had ended, the Panzerwaffe still existed, but not as the offensive weapon they were in the early Blitzkrieg years.

Nobody could deny that the assault gun proved itself to be a decisive weapon on the battlefield. In the first years of the war it had been an effective offensive weapon protecting the infantry from enemy tank units and clearing a path for them to advance. However, as the war changed the assault gun was compelled to evolve into that of a tank destroyer. Despite great success in action, the StuG was unable to overcome the huge array of Russian armour, and as a consequence incurred high losses.

But in spite the massive losses sustained the assault gun crews had won a reputation for daring and professionalism in combat. The titanic struggles which had been placed upon them during the war in Russia and on the Western Front provided the very backbone of Germany's armoured and infantry defence until the very end of the war.

Another photograph of a Bulgarian Maybach T-III probably during anti-partisan operations in the Balkans in mid-1944. During that period the Germans sent a substantial quantity of armour to the area in an attempt to defend from advancing Red Army forces.

A close-up view of a Bulgarian Maybach T-III moving across uneven terrain during operations in the Balkans in 1944. Some fifty assault guns and eighty-eight Pz.Kpfw.IVs were placed at the disposal of the Bulgarian Army.

This page and opposite: Four photographs apparently showing the same Bulgarian Maybach T-III (StuG.III.Ausf.G). The vehicle registration number 'B60537' can quite clearly be indentified on both the rear and front plates of the assault gun. The St. Andrew's Cross is painted in black and indicates that this vehicle is a attached a Bulgarian *Sturmgeschütz* unit.

Panzergrenadiers wearing their distinctive winter reversible's white side-out have hitched a lift on board a whitewashed assault gun during the winter of 1944. Even as the war approached it's end a number of assault gun units continued to spearhead the German armoured assault in a number of places.

An interesting photograph showing an Ausf.G variant with what appears to be a concrete-reinforced frontal superstructure. Note how the crew has camouflaged part of the hull and bottom part of the 7.5cm StuK40 L/48 gun barrel.

A late variant StuG.III.Ausf.G during operations in Army Group Centre in the summer of 1944, possibly during 'Operation Bagration'. Of interest is the layer of concrete on the front of the casemate in order give the vehicle additional armoured protection.

An Ausf.G moving along a road to the battle front in the autumn of 1944. Tank track links can be seen bolted to the casemate front plates. The vehicle has early type side skirting armour attached.

An assault gun has become stuck in muddy water and a halftrack is attempting to pull the stricken vehicle out of the mire using the StuGs tow cables.

Crewman can be seen on their StuG.IV moving along a dusty road. Track links can be seen attached to the vehicle for additional armoured protection. Note the protective covering placed on the end of the 7.5cm guns muzzle break to prevent dust particles and other foreign matter contaminating the gun tube.

Three assault guns cross a field and drive on to a dusty road. Whilst the StuG was regarded as an effective weapon against the mighty Red Army, the open terrain coupled with inadequate support caused unprecedented amounts of losses both on the Eastern and Western Fronts.

A StuG.III.Ausf.G motors forward towards the battle front somewhere in the West in autumn of 1944. Note the kill rings on the 7.5cm StuK40 L/48 gun barrel. Foliage has also been applied to the vehicle to help reduce aerial detection.

By the appearance of the taut towing cable this Ausf.G is towing another vehicle somewhere on the *Ost* front in 1944. Note the missing side skirt plates.

A stationary Ausf.G is parked inside a fortified town possibly in Germany in early 1945. The vehicles unit insignia indicates that it belongs to the StuG.Abt.600. The tactical number '131' is painted in yellow next to the national cross on the intact armoured side skirting.

An excellent view of an Ausf.G advancing along a road with a tarpaulin protecting the vehicle from the rain. For the Panzerwaffe fighting for survival on the Eastern Front shortages of every kind was affecting most of the old and experienced assault gun units. The Soviets had unmatchable material superiority, and yet, despite this major drawback in late 1944 armoured vehicle production, including tanks, assault guns, and self-propelled assault guns, were higher than in any month before May 1944.

An Ausf.G supporting infantry during operations. Whilst this scene appears like it could be in northern Italy, the photograph was probably taken in southern Russia during Army Group South's withdrawal.

An assault gun crew pose for the camera in front of their vehicle somewhere in northern Italy in 1944. Even in Italy assault gun units fought fearlessly against the overwhelming might of the Anglo-American forces, and in some areas of the front actually thwarted their drive through the country.

Two assault guns in a decimated town during the last year of the war on the Eastern Front. Although *Sturmgeschütz* commanders were fully aware of the fruitless attempts by its units to establish a defensive line, the crews followed instructions implicitly in a number of areas to halt the Soviet drive. Again and again the StuG fought to the grim death.

More than likely taken from a captured cine film this picture shows a StuG bound for the front. Of interest, note the different side skirts attached to the vehicle, more than likely cannibalised from another assault gun. One side skirt plate has a dark yellow sand base with a camouflage scheme of red and brown and olive green patches, whilst the other plate is painted in simple sand base with much of the camouflage paint scheme missing.

Here an excellent photo of a hybrid vehicle based on the StuG.III.Ausf.G. The superstructure was mounted on a Pz.Kpfw.H or J chassis, which was designated for the StuG.IV assault gun. In this photograph it shows one of those hybrid StuGs attached to the 4.SS.Panzer-Division 'Polizei' on the Eastern Front in 1944.

An Ausf.G variant rolls along a road in Silesia in late March 1945. The crew have expertly applied lots of foliage over the vehicle whilst driving during daylight hours. Note there is only one piece of side skirt left on the right side.

A wrecked assault gun sits at the side of the road as a grim reminder of the terrible cost of these vehicles during defensive operations in the East.

Here an assault gun crew can be seen sitting on their StuG.III.Ausf.G whilst being transported by rail to the front lines during the summer of 1944.

A commanding officer can be seen standing on top of a StuG.IV addresses his troops during a ceremony. The vehicle has intact side skirts and a tactical number '21' painted in red with a white outline. The 7.5cm StuK40 muzzle break has protective covering.

Two photographs taken in sequence showing a knocked out assault gun in the ruins of a post war Berlin. For the remaining StuGs that had fought inside the doomed *Reich* capital in April 1945, there had been hardly enough assault guns and other armour to stem the mighty Red Army, but even so courageous crews fought on ceaselessly trying to prolong the death throes of the *Panzerwaffe*.

Three photographs taken in sequence showing a StuG.III.Ausf.G with their crew next to a repair shed. One of the vehicles in the photograph appears to be a captured British armoured vehicle. The assault gun has been given an application of zimmerit anti-magnetic mine paste.

The crew of an Ausf.G prepare to move their vehicle out of cover. They have already removed most of the foliage and are now in the process of removing the tarpaulin. The vehicle is finished in a base colour of dark yellow, which has been given a coat of winter whitewash paint.

A knocked out assault gun lays at the side of the road after evidently becoming embroiled in a heavy fire fight. Throughout the later period of the war the StuG continued to provide its worth as an invaluable anti-tank weapon. Yet, in spite the huge losses, in a number of last ditch battles it showed its true capabilities as a tank killer.

An interesting photograph showing a StuG.III.Ausf.G re-designated as an assault howitzer in order to help counter the growing might of the Red Army weaponry. The vehicle has an application of zimmerit anti-magnetic mine paste over its superstructure and has missing side skirting, more than likely knocked out during an enemy contact.

Infantry using a StuG.III.Ausf.G for vital support during the late winter of 1944. Whilst a number of soldiers can be seen hitching a lift on the engine deck of the vehicle there are other soldiers that can be seen in a slit trench. By the appearance of the infantry it is evident that the enemy have been located further along the road and appear to be taking cover.

An excellent photo of a whitewashed Ausf.G with attached smoke candle dischargers on the forward edge of the casemate. One of the crewmen can be seen with his MG34 behind his splinter shield, while a pair of infantry men occupies the engine deck.

A stationary whitewashed StuG.III.Ausf.G with missing side skirts can be seen in a muddy field. The vehicle has an application of zimmerit anti-magnetic mine-paste. In September 1944 zimmerit was discontinued as there were concerns that it was inflammable under the impact of projectiles.

Two assault gun crews wearing a variety of issue and non issue army clothing stand next to their StuG in early 1945 inside a forest. The whitewashed assault gun is fully loaded with supplies that can be seen stowed on the engine deck.

An Ausf.G moves along a road carrying a dispatch rider's motorcycle on the near track-guard. Note the markings on the superstructure rear plate, which is a sign for a tracked, self-propelled *Panzerjäger* unit.

An interesting photograph showing a column of Ausf.G's halted on the outskirts of a village somewhere in the East. The leading vehicle has special Ost tracks fitted to the vehicle in order to give it better manoeuvrability across the often uneven and perilous terrain.

A column of dejected German PoWs march past a knocked out StuG.IV probably in eastern Germany or along the borders of Poland in early February or March 1945. By February 1945 German forces in the East had been driven back to the River Oder, the last stronghold of defence before Berlin.

Soviet troops occupy a decimated town in eastern Germany in March 1945. A StuG.IV has been knocked out in the urbanized battle. Although the last remaining Sturmgeschütz units saw extensive action, its success was limited and localized and did nothing to avert enemy operations.

Children can be seen playing near a StuG.III.Ausf.G in decimated Berlin immediately after the fall of the Reich capital in May 1945. By the visible appearance of the vehicle it is quite evident that the assault has been knocked out of action by anti-tank rounds.

An abandoned StuG.III's in the early spring of 1945. During the last two years of the war the StuG was gradually called upon for offensive and defensive fire support, where it was gradually embroiled in an anti-tank role trying to stem the might of the Red Army. During the last weeks of the war as fuel and spare parts became scarce many StuG's were either destroyed or simply abandoned by the crews.

Camouflage and Zimmerit

When the Germans unleashed its might against France in 1940, all the assault guns were painted in dark grey. Even one year later when the Germans first attacked Russia the StuGs still retained their own grey colour scheme. For the first four months of operation 'Barbarossa', the vehicles remained painted in their overall dark grey camouflage scheme and blended well against the local terrain. However, with the drastic onset of winter and the first snow showers at the end of October 1941, assault gun crews would soon be filled with anxiety, as their vehicles were not camouflaged for winter warfare. With the worrying prospects of fighting in Russia in the snow the *Wehrmacht* reluctantly issued washable white winter camouflage paint in November 1941. The paint was specially designed to be thinned with water and applied to all vehicles and equipment where snow was on the ground. The application of this new winter white wash paint could easily be washed off by the crews in the spring, exposing the dark grey base colour. Unfortunately for the crews the order came too late and the distribution to the front lines was delayed by weeks. Consequently, the crews had to adapt and find various crude substitutes to camouflage their vehicles. This included hastily applying their vehicles with a rough coat of lime white wash, whilst others used lumps of chalk, white cloth strips and sheets, and even hand-packed snow in a drastic attempt to conceal conspicuous dark grey parts. Other vehicles, however, roamed the white arctic wilderness with no camouflage at all.

Following the harsh winter of 1941, the spring of 1942 saw the return of the dark grey base colour on all the vehicles. It was during this period that a number of assault guns saw the return of pre-war dark brown and dark green camouflage schemes. Crews had learnt from the previous year the lessons of camouflage and survival for these young men were paramount. For this reason many crews begun utilizing and adding to their camouflage schemes by finding various substitutes and applying them to the surface of the vehicle. This included the wide spread use of foliage and bundles of grass and hay. This was a particularly effective method and was often used to break up the distinctive shapes and allow them to blend into the local terrain. Mud too was used as an effective form of camouflage but was never universally appreciated among the crews.

For the first time in southern Russia, in the Crimea and the Caucasus, where the summer weather was similar to that in North Africa, many vehicles were given an application of tropical camouflage, with the widespread use of sand colour schemes, almost identical to those used in the *Afrika-Korps*. In southern Russia in the summer the terrain was very similar to that of a desert and for that reason the vehicles were completed in the tropical colours of yellow brown RAL 8000 grey green RAL 7008 or just brown RAL 8017.

By 1943, olive green was being used on vehicles, weapons, and large pieces of equipment. A Red brown colour RAL 8012 also had been introduced at the same time. These two colours, along with a new colour base of dark yellow RAL 7028 were issued to crews in the form a high concentrated paste. The paste arrived in 2kg and 20kg cans, and units were ordered to apply these cans of coloured paste over the entire surface of the vehicle. The paste was specially adapted so that it could be thinned with water or even fuel, and could be applied by spray, brush, or mop.

The dark yellow paste was issued primarily to cover unwanted colours or areas of the camouflage schemes, especially during changes in seasons. These new variations of colours gave the crews the widest possible choices in schemes so as to blend in as much as possible to the local terrain. The pastes were also used to colour all canvas tops and tarpaulins on the vehicles.

The new three-colour paint scheme worked very well on the front lines and allowed each unit maximum advantage, depending on the surrounding conditions. However, within months there were frequent problems with supply. Support vehicles carrying the new paste had to travel so far to various scattered units, even from railheads, that frequently the assault gun units never received any new application of camouflage schemes. Another problem was due to the fact that many StuG units were already heavily embroiled in bitter fighting and had neither the vehicles to spare nor manpower to pull them out for a repaint. Even rear area ordnance workshops were returning vehicles to action at such speed that they only managed time to replace parts, and then send them back to the front with no repaint. A great many number of vehicles never received any paste colours at all, and those that fought on remained in dark yellow, sometimes with crews adapting and enhancing the scheme with the application of foliage and mud.

However, of all the failings, the greatest of them all was actually the paints themselves. These proved to be unstable when mixed with water, and even the lightest down pour could cause these new colours to run or wash off the vehicles. Even fuel, which was used to give the paste a durable finish, was at such a premium during the later stages of the war, that units were compelled to use water, waste oil and mixed or other paints. All this caused immense variations in the appearance of the paint schemes and as a consequence there were unusual colours like brick red, chocolate brown and light green. In spite of these variations in colour and the fact that there had become little standardization in the camouflage schemes, occasionally though there were complete units that appeared on the front lines properly painted and marked. But this was often a rare occurrence, especially by 1944.

Throughout 1944, a further drain on German supplies and resources caused considerable disruption of materials. The paint system on the vehicles was just one of many hundreds of deprivations that were inflicted on the already badly depleted assault gun units. During the last months of 1944, the Panzer supply became critical and lots of vehicles were seen in overall dark yellow.

By this time almost all the new vehicles that had left the last remaining factories for the front lines were in their base colour dark yellow. They never received any further camouflage treatment, other than covering with foliage.

The use of foliage during the last years of the war was extensive. Most vehicles and a large range of weapons attached foliage to break up the distinctive shapes. The Germans were masters in the art of camouflaging their vehicles with branches from trees, grass and hay. In fact, some vehicles carried so much foliage that it was sometimes difficult to determine what type of vehicle they were or what camouflage scheme it had. In the last furious year of the war, foliage had become more important than colours. To the crews being concealed from aerial attack was the key to survival. As the remnants of the once vaunted Panzer divisions withdrew across Poland to the borders of the Reich the crews did not dare waste any time painting vehicles. The widespread use of foliage helped compensate for this.

Typical Assault Gun Unit November 1942

Three Batteries of the Ten Guns Each

Chief Unit

Staff (One Assault Gun III)
Staff Battery with Leader's Group
Intelligence Troop
Supply Service
Medical Service
Repair Service
Replacement Group
Rescue Troop
Battery Supply Train
Unit Food Services

1st Assault Gun Battery

Leader Group (1 Assault Gun III)
Combat Battery
Gun Crew (3 Platoons with 3 guns each)
Ammunition Troop
Vehicle Repair Troop
Battery Supply Train

2nd Assault Gun Battery

Leader Group (1 Assault Gun III)
Combat Battery

Gun Crew (3 Platoons with 3 guns each)
Ammunition Troop
Vehicle Repair Troop
Battery Supply Train

3rd Assault Gun Battery

Leader Group (1 Assault Gun III)
Combat Battery
Gun Crew (3 Platoons with 3 guns each)
Ammunition Troop
Vehicle Repair Troop
Battery Supply Train

Standard StuG.III Variants

StuG III Ausf.A
The first version of the StuG (the Ausf.A) entered service just in time to take part in the campaign in the west in May-June 1940.
Number produced:
5 prototypes 1937,
30 1 Serie, January-May 1940
Length: 5.38m
Hull Width: 2.92m
Height: 1.95m
Crew: 4
Weight: 19.6 tons
Engine: 320hp Maybach HL120TR
Max Speed: 40km/hr
Max Range: 160km/
Main Armament: One 7.5cm StuK37 L/24

StuG III Ausf.B
The StuG III Ausf.B was very similar to the Ausf A, but with wider 40cm tracks in place of the 36cm tracks used on the earlier model.
Number produced: 320
Produced: June 1940-May 1941

Length: 5.40m
Hull Width: 2.93m
Height: 1.98m
Crew: 4
Weight: 20.2 tons
Engine: 320hp Maybach HL120TRM
Max Speed: 40km/hr
Max Range: 160km/
Main Armament: One 7.5cm StuK37 L/24

StuG III Ausf.C

The StuG III Ausf.C saw the introduction of a periscopic gun sight in place of the direct vision sight used on earlier machines.
Number produced: 50
Produced: May-September 1941
Length: 5.40m
Hull Width: 2.93m
Height: 1.98m
Crew: 4
Weight: 20.2 tons
Engine: 320hp Maybach HL120TRM
Max Speed: 40km/hr
Max Range: 160km/
Main Armament: One 7.5cm StuK37 L/24

StuG III Ausf.D

The StuG III Ausf.D was virtually identical to the Ausf.C, with no visual differences. Internally a bell was added to help the commander get the attention of the driver. It is possible that this version of the StuG saw the introduction of face hardened armour.
Number produced: 150
Produced: May-September 1941
Length: 5.40m
Hull Width: 2.93m
Height: 1.98m
Crew: 4
Weight: 20.2 tons
Engine: 320hp Maybach HL120TRM

Max Speed: 40km/hr
Max Range: 160km/
Main Armament: One 7.5cm StuK37 L/24

StuG III Ausf.E

The StuG III Ausf.E was the final version of the machine to carry the short gun. The main change made from the Ausf.D was an increase in the size of the armoured pannier on the left of the superstructure and the addition of a new pannier on the right, increasing the storage space and making it easier to use the StuG as a command vehicle.

Number produced: 272
Produced: September 1941-March 1942
Length: 5.40m
Hull Width: 2.93m
Height: 1.98m
Crew: 4
Weight: 20.8 tons
Engine: 320hp Maybach HL120TRM
Max Speed: 40km/hr
Max Range: 160km/
Main Armament: One 7.5cm StuK37 L/24
Machine Gun: One 7.92mm MG34

StuG III Ausf.F

The StuG III Ausf.F saw the introduction of the 7.5cm StuK40 L/43 gun. With its higher muzzle velocity and armour piercing ammunition this gun turned the StuG into a potent tank killer.

Number produced: 359
Produced: March-September 1942
Length: 6.31m (with L/43 gun)
Hull Width: 2.92m
Height: 2.15m
Crew: 4
Weight: 21.6 tons
Engine: 320hp Maybach HL120TRM
Max Speed: 40km/hr
Max Range: 140km/
Main Armament: One 7.5cm StuK40 L/43 or L/48to

Machine Guns: One 7.92mm MG34

StuG III Ausf.F/8

The StuG III Ausf.F/8 was similar to the Ausf.F, but used the improved hull developed for the Panzer III Ausf.J, in the first change to the basic hull design of the StuG since it was introduced.
Number produced: 334
Produced: September-December 1942
Length: 6.77m
Hull Width: 2.92m
Height: 2.15m
Crew: 4
Weight: 23.2 tons
Engine: 320hp Maybach HL120TRM
Max Speed: 40km/hr
Max Range: 140km/
Main Armament: One 7.5cm StuK40 L/48
Machine Guns: One 7.92mm MG34

StuG III Ausf G

The StuG III Ausf.G was the final production version of the StuG. With a total of 7,720 built from new between December 1942 and the end of the Second World War it was produced in larger numbers than any other version of any German tank. It featured an improved superstructure with sloped side armour, and a commander's cupola was added to the top of the fighting compartment.
Number produced: 7,720
Produced: December 1942-March 1945
Length: 6.77m
Hull Width: 2.95m
Height: 2.16m
Crew: 4
Weight: 23.9 tons
Engine: 320hp Maybach HL120TRM
Max Speed: 40km/hr
Max Range: 155km/ 95 miles
Main Armament: One 7.5cm StuK40 L/48
Machine Guns: One to three 7.92mm MG34 or MG42

Sturmgeschütz Units in the Waffen-SS

Divisions

1. Leibstandarte SS Adolf Hitler
Leibstandarte SS Adolf Hitler (1 Sep 1939 – 13 Aug 1940)
V. Batallion
Sturmartillerie-Batterie – (6x StuG)
Leibstandarte SS Adolf Hitler (mot) (13 Aug 1940 – 15 July 1942)
Abteilung Schönberger
1. Sturmgeschütz-Batterie
1. Batterie – (7x StuG III 7.5cm)
2. Batterie – (7x StuG III 7.5cm)
3. Batterie – (7x StuG III 7.5cm)
SS-Division (mot.) Leibstandarte SS Adolf Hitler (15 July 1942 – 22 Oct 1942)
Sturmgeschütz-Abteilung (Brigade)
Stabs – (1x StuG III 7.5cm)
1. Batterie – (9x StuG III 7.5cm)
2. Batterie – (9x StuG III 7.5cm)
3. Batterie – (9x StuG III 7.5cm)
SS-Panzergrenadier-Division Leibstandarte SS Adolf Hitler (22 Oct 1942 – 22 Oct 1943)
Sturmgeschütz-Abteilung
Stabs – (1x StuG III 7.5cm)
1. Batterie – (10x StuG III 7.5cm)
2. Batterie – (10x StuG III 7.5cm)
3. Batterie – (10x StuG III 7.5cm)

2.SS Das Reich
SS-Division Reich (mot) – (1941–1942)

Sturmgeschütz Batterie (6x StuG)
SS-Panzergrenadier-Division Das Reich – (1942–1943)
Sturmgeschütz Abteilung 2. (Das Reich)
Stabs – (3x StuG III 7.5cm)
1. Batterie – (10x StuG III 7.5cm)
2. Batterie – (10x StuG III 7.5cm)
3. Batterie – (10x StuG III 7.5cm)
2. SS-Panzer Division Das Reich – (1943–1944)
2. SS-Sturmgeschütz Abteilung
Stabs – (3x StuG III 7.5cm)
1. Batterie – (10x StuG III 7.5cm)
2. Batterie – (10x StuG III 7.5cm)